Unspoken Words, Beautifully Written
Neter Ankh Hotep-El

Soul Rhymer Productions

Published by Nah El Publications
1255 Race Track Road
Sumter, S.C. 29153

Cover design by Neterankhhotep-El for Soul Rhymer Productions

All rights reserved. No part of this publication may be reproduced, stored in a retrieval system, or transmitted in any form or by any means, electronic, mechanical, including photocopying, recording, or otherwise, without the written permission of the publisher.

Copyright © 2015 Unspoken Words, Beautifully Written by Neterankhhotep-El
ISBN 978-0-9969851-0-9

Dedication

To my mother Frances
To my father Donald
To my brother Derrick
To my sister in law Leah
To my niece Daniele
To my nephew Christopher
To all my beloved family
By way of blood, spirit and pen.

Acknowledgements

Over five years ago I embarked on a mission to have a collection of my poems published. What came forth was a book titled, "Chaotic Love" which due to the printing company I went through and a lack of marketing on my behalf, led to a not so successful mission. With a passion and desire to get back to writing and manifest some lost works, I embarked on a new mission and now I'm offering to the world some of my finest poems.

Table of Contents

Echoes From The Ancients 1
The Love Letter 3
A Little Song 5
My Head Is Nappy 6
Days At The Plantation 8
Black Super Hero 10
Thievery 12
The Tear That Didn't Drop 14
Leave Your Love 15
Just Right 17
I'm Loving Me 18
In Your Eyes 20
Her Eyes Spoke To Me 21
Eyes On You 23
This Black Skin 25
My Soul Glows 28
What Happened To Us 30
Dreamy Nights We Share 32
I Fell In Love 33
A Day Of Remembrance 34
Epiphany 36
Creativity Is Important In Education 38
Friendship 40
In Memory Of You 41
Twin Soul Mates 42
Loving You From Afar 43

A Brother Forgotten 46
Is It Alright If I Cry 48
I'm Tired Y'all 49
When Kisses Were Cherished 51
Teach Me 53
Let's Do It 54
She Is So Beautiful 56
Ma 57
I Want To Make You Smile 58
Sun Worshippers 60
His Wife Of Mine 62
This Thing Called Love 64
Alone In A Crowded Room 65
I Care 66
Bring Me A Dream 67
I Live 69
I Need What You Want 70

About The Author 74

Echoes From The Ancients

I hear echoes from the ancients
But it's more like cries and pleas,
Saying to beware of the times
When lives are consumed by lies and greed.
Civilizations flourish and perish
As history repeats itself,
In the end all great nations
Submit to death.
I hear echoes from the ancients
Sounding like whispers in the wind,
Or the rain drops that fall
On the roofs made of tin.
The echoes... the echoes...
Echoes from the ancients,
Saying our future isn't written in stone
At anytime we can change it.
Peace will never be attain by war
When the conquered hearts are hardened,
Karma, karma, karma
From this no action is pardoned.
I hear echoes from the ancients
Words of wisdom from the old,
Prophecies written on papyrus
Sacred texts written on scrolls.
Love more and love unconditionally
Life is a school to perfect the soul,
Laugh more and laugh more my child

May your laughter be ever bold.
I hear echoes from the ancients
Questions falling upon my ears,
What legacy will I leave behind?
What have I accomplished throughout the years?
What are my offerings to the world?
Did I contribute to its healing?
Or did I cause harm and suffering?
Did I find pain appealing?
I hear echoes from the ancients
Spread peace and have compassion,
Shed light unto the path
For all those in your passing.
Yes, peace, love and light
On your journey, these must you carry,
Go now my son in all the worlds
Go on and do not tarry.

The Love Letter

Dear Beloved,
I seem to have fallen madly in love with you,
I assure you I've questioned the legitimacy of it myself
But nevertheless these words are true.
You see My Darling, thoughts of you
They seem to permeate my mind,
And I find myself engaged for countless hours
Unaware of the passing of time.
What a spell I'm under perhaps
But oh how I do enjoy it so,
You see I never remember flowers smelling so wonderful
As I'm walking to and fro.
The birds sing songs that enchant my ears
My heart has become light as a feather,
As I stroll along the forest's edge
It too brings much pleasure.
If this is not love what could it be?
Is it insanity I suffer?
Is it lunacy that my appetite's suppressed
And I have not a taste for supper?
Forgive me for my ramblings
The tongue incoherently conveys the mind's thought,
Slow is the coordination of the body after all
In relations to divine sorts.
But no longer will I consume your time
With these murmurs of my heart,

Hoping these words have fan the flames
Or at least ignited a spark.

A Little Song

Overwhelmed by the waves your eyes fashioned
Cast into the sea like a ship sunken,
For I am crew members with no captain
Amidst the lightning's crackling and rumblings.
To passionately kiss thy lips I dream
To taste the most sweetest of all nectars,
From your fountain within, such running streams
Just one sip gives rise to life forever.
With admiration the sun adorns you
For your smile is a companion of his,
Your radiance, it falls like morning dew
Men scurry for its perpetual bliss.
Rich smells of ambrosia fills the air
As the wind gently caresses your skin,
Another woman surely can't compare
With the beauty thou possess from within.
My heart's desire, to be loved by thee,
To be yours forever and filled with glee.

My Head Is Nappy

My head is nappy but my soul is happy.

These words I heard my father utter many mornings like a mantra.
In the bathroom picking his afro
The four walls couldn't conceal his black soul.
His deep strong voice
With an accent of New York.

My head is nappy but my soul is happy.

The soulful sounds like a southern singer
Put me in the mind of James Brown.
The godfather as my father
Stepped from the bathroom like he stepped from a barber.
His afro aesthetics was nothing short of amazing
He picked and sheen, picked and sheen,
Can you picture the scene?
He picked and shine!
An afro perfectly shaped as if molded by the gods
Say it loud!

My head is nappy but my soul is happy.
My head is nappy but my soul is happy.

These words reinforced later convictions

Of nappiness equates with happiness.
The more nappier I am, the more happier I am.
In other words,
I'm at my happiest when I'm nappiest.
Who needs relaxers?
Why should I relax?
Everything that grows reaches toward heaven
So do my naps.
Let it stretch forth to its' max.
These same naps, kinks and curls
They spiral,
The same way the galaxy does
That's why my hair's rivaled.
Afros, braids and locs,
Nappy headed men and women on the block.
I hear them say

My head is nappy but my soul is happy.

Days At The Plantation

Mornings before the sunrise
I rise from my slumber,
My eyes feeling deprived
You can tell as I stumble.
Mumbling words of motivation
In preparation of my day,
Throughout the hallway I sway
For my chariot I pray.
To swing lo and behold
My face in the mirror,
I go out to face the world
As the world face a nigger.
Sun up to sun down
Am I toiling for change?
I hear my ancestors calling
But you're calling me strange.
The chains have been moved
From our body to mind,
On the mountain top is freedom
But they don't allow you to climb.
In the confines of a building
But it's destroying our soul,
We're slaving for paper
While they're hoarding the gold.
Separated from family
Investing time in the matrix,

Hoping for a vacation
To restore the time that we wasted.

Black Super Hero

No cape
No "S" on my chest,
But still I'm god in the flesh.
Black super hero.
All black
From my head to my toes,
And I shine like the sun
I glow.
Black super hero.
Knotty locs like a
Ras-ta-far-I,
I came from the stars
Out the sky.
Black super hero.
Any problem
It's my duty to solve them,
That's why I'm called a
Black super hero.
Don't you hesitate
Just call me when you need me,
I'll be on my way
Like how a summer's breeze be.
And the bumble bees be
I'm a seed of greatness!
Often I walk light
But I still crack pavements.

Like a black rose, far from black prose
See my black soul is like a black hole
In the black abyss,
Pump a black fist.
Put a peace sign in the air
And I'll be there.
To cease the violence
My weapons are love, wisdom and kindness.
My ancestors were warriors and
It is their blood that travel my veins,
Descendants of kings are the melodies that birds sing.
I understand.
Heroes can be traced back to Heru
The son of Ausar and Auset,
When he avenged his father's death
When he took up arms and fought Set.
Black super Heru.
Every day that I avoid incarceration or extermination
I wipe off the perspiration,
And after a few exhalations
I look in the mirror with admiration
Knowing that I have given others inspiration.
And I say to myself
You black super hero.

Thievery

She came like a thief in the night
Full of deception, prone to cunning,
Dressed in black from head to toes
Beautiful and truly stunning.
Her first theft was my attention
Undivided when first sighted,
Captivated by her every move
And sure to lose if I tried to fight it.
Her second theft was my breath
She took it away quite quickly,
The sweet smell of her fragrance lingered
Ever so light, yet richly.
The scent of a thousand roses
With the addition of sweet basil,
Or per chance the concoction of rain in the forest
With just a hint of maple.
Her third theft was my beating heart
Pounding fast as drums producing trance,
A daughter of an Aztec I suppose
As my life was in her hands.
I stood like an empty vessel
A puppet of hers on strings,
My head in the clouds with an angelic being
I was wrapped inside her wings.
Her fourth theft was time itself
As it sat still and frozen,

Forever flew in the wind like sand
As if an hourglass was broken.
Her fifth theft was anticipated
And anxiously I waited,
For the time will come she would steal a kiss
And this theft would be my favorite.

The Tear That Didn't Drop

Last night I cried
Because my heart was filled with pain,
My eyes were all watery
Then the tears they came.
One fell and hit the floor
Shattering just like glass,
Where they landed didn't baffle me
Not a one but the last.
As I sat there just a waiting
Pondering where it might fall,
Or perhaps the path it may take upon my cheek
But it didn't move at all.
I waited for its' fall
At that time it didn't matter where,
But as I sat there just a waiting
It also sat just there.

Leave Your Love

*I never thought I'd feel this way
I promised myself I wouldn't,
I vowed until this forgotten day
To love again, I shouldn't.
But I find myself now letting go
Of the barriers that surrounded my heart,
As I lay down my guards at a moderate slow
I brace myself for the start.
The beginning of a new road to travel
Or perhaps an old road with a new beginning,
As I begin to journey my mind unravels
This could be a new beginning with an old ending.
My heart was shattered some times before
Even I had experienced some lost,
And all this just goes to show
That the price of love does cost.
But whenever you are near my dear
My heartbeat increase indeed,
Or either it skips a beat because it's clear
That you're everything I need.
From your smile to your laugh
That's exactly what I'm missing,
Badly I need you to be my better half
That's exactly what I'm wishing.
The mother of my son and daughter
Also the lady of my dreams,*

The course taken by flowing water
Developing from a stream.
I want to share happiness with you
So I can be complete,
I haven't shown you what I can do
And how I can be so sweet.
If the universe allows and time permits
You'll get the chance to see it,
And if happiness can start with one kiss
Then we'll get the chance to be it.
And if for some reason we should part
Just take a look above,
Take my pride, take my joy and take my heart
But please, just leave your love.

Just Right

Today when I awoke I felt revived
I guess I slept well last night,
I received sufficient rest not more
Not less, I guess just right.
I went outside for some air
And the breezes were so light,
The wind blew but not so hard
Perhaps to say just right.
The sky was a pretty hue of blue
And the sun shined so bright,
The rays danced round about my face
Not vigorously but just right.
Birds everywhere seemed energized
And immediately took flight,
Soaring through the blue filled sky
Not too high or low but just right.
The grass was the prettiest green I've seen
It was such a sight,
So soft to the tender soles of my feet
Ah, it was just right.

I'm Loving Me

L-O-V-E
I'm loving me unconditionally.
I will not take heed to your opinion
Because my self esteem is "my" self esteem.
I blow off steam like an iron
Strong I am like a lion,
My pride is my pride
My eyes are on Zion.
I've climbed mountains as high as Everest
And the Himalayas,
In the realm of my mind
Sending forth prayers, of love.
I'm loving me
As I never loved before,
Flaws and all
So when I walk out that door
I'm saying hey young world
I'm the reflection of perfection.
My smile is bright as the sun
And beautiful as the sun setting.
The clothes that I'm wearing
Do not define my essence,
My essence is that of the divine
And I'm wrapped in blessings.
I'm never less than but equal to greatness
Is what I'm professing,

I'm loving me, I'm loving me, I'm loving me.
I am a walking contradiction
To your logistics,
I am common sense not so common
Commonly called mystic.
Mistake me not for one willing to participate
In your theatrics,
I have prior engagements on the stage
In my world where I'm the actor and the actress.
I'm loving me is the title of the play
Written, directed and produced by yours truly.
I'm loving me as I never loved before,
I'm going deep down within, deep as the ocean's floor.
I'm just scratching the surface when i say
That I'm searching for myself,
A new me, a better me
Something beyond flesh.
No reality show can show my reality
And that's real,
And no radio station can broadcast
Exactly how I feel.
I am happy, I am love
I am in love, I am free,
I'm loving me, I'm loving me
I'm loving me.

In Your Eyes

When I look into your eyes, I see a soul hurt.
So much pain that it has endured.
So many prayers that has been prayed
For the day the soul to be cured.
When I look into your eyes, I see a young girl
With a heart as big as the sun,
Whose love can warm the entire planet
And plus some additional ones.
When I look into your eyes, I see so much
Without a spoken word,
Like pages of books upon your pupils
I see nouns, adjectives and verbs.
When I look into your eyes, I see so much
But you only asked for a little,
A little time, patience, hope and love
A little hug, kiss and giggle.

Her Eyes Spoke To Me

It wasn't her breasts, that stood so firm that if she took
Off her bra they would only drop a few degrees like before rain,
It wasn't the fact that her bubble in the back could make
you double back and struggle to ask for her phone number
while forgetting your own name.
Yeah, her lips might have been juicy enough to seduce me
Or make me sweat profusely and truthfully,
As a man I noticed all three
But it was the fourth one that caught me.
Hook, line and sinker you shouldn't tinker
With what you call destiny and fate,
But as I gazed upon her face
It was as if her eyes had something to say.
At first glance it seemed innocent
But her eyes spoke, "Look closer."
Her eyes whispered, "Can you see it?"
Then the room got colder.
They say beauty is in the eyes of the beholder
But have you ever beheld the eyes of someone beautiful?
Her eyes spoke to me.
Whispering to me all the moments she cried
For being yelled at.
For all the moments she contemplated suicide
But on the outside you couldn't tell that.
You couldn't tell that her boyfriend sells crack

And once she had to sell herself and ever since then she felt bad.
Her eyes spoke to me.
They told stories of abuse and how mechanisms were produced to override the discomfort brought forth by the accused,
Who was never publicly accused but only in the mind because she refused to be out casted by family
And ridiculed.
Her eyes spoke to me.
Of the true love she often seek,
No one showed her how to be a woman so she pieced together some ideas from t.v.
From listening to songs on her mp3
She thought every man wanted a woman to be bi-sexual,
I was hoping my eyes spoke to hers so when she asked, "What should she try to be?" Mine replied, "Try special."
Her eyes spoke to me.
Thanking me for seeing beyond her physical body.
Thanking me for seeing her soul.

Eyes On You

From the moment I laid eyes on you
Beautiful, pretty, sexy and fine came to mind,
You're a carbon based being, refined coal
You're a diamond that shines.
You were fashioned by the hands of god
Khnum knows what I'm speaking of,
You're the reason men seek love
Some get caught up in the lust.
I want to be caught up in your clutch
When you pass by my adrenaline rush,
If my heart could speak each beat would say something like
I'm dying for your touch.
Your strength is amazing so it hurts me
Seeing a tear fall from your face,
I'll go through hell to make sure heaven is yours
That was my fall from grace.
A taste of your lips is the elixir to life
I'm talking ambrosia and libations,
Sensual sensations
Unresistable temptations.
Beyond courageous with all due praises.
Your reflections is like the moon when it goes through phases,
I flow with phrases.
Poetical sentences.
Sentence me to the confines of your unconditional love

With no censorship.
Anticipations of visitations and conversations
Our vibrations,
Little creations of palpations, in my heart chakra.
You feel that?
I think I may need a doctor or nurse
This moment here was the reason for my birth.
From the moment I laid eyes on you
I couldn't picture a better vision,
Frozen in time your pupils
Became my prison.

This Black Skin

This black skin
The fusion of melanin
There's something extragalactic about it.
Even the Universe strut her hips like
You don't see all this?
It's all about this black skin I'm in.
From adoration to condemnation
And back at adoration.
This is God's creation at its' finest!
Diamonds envy because
They just aren't cutting it,
What are you really talking about
If you're not discussing it?
This black skin that is.
Dipped in chocolate and sun kissed
Often imitated and you know the rest,
This is what stars look like
Wrapped in flesh.
I'm proud to be coated
With something better than gold,
I am a treasure chest filled with treasures
That cannot corrode.
I don't grow old.
I defy aging, I am greatness!
I defy gravity like spaceships.
I'm fly.

This black skin is why.
But this black skin...

I remember whips cutting through this black skin
Like a hot knife through butter,
This black skin covered in blood
As it's slumped in a puddle.
The struggle of dying to be free
Way past trying to be free,
One day I'll be liberated
Catching myself, lying to me.
This black skin has been branded
The hot iron that left it damaged,
You seen tissue falling to the waste side
Like masons chipping at granite.
No matter how hard I scrub
This black skin can't be exfoliated,
This black skin is the sole reason I'm hated.
Poor little black me
As they pour tar and feather me,
Maybe I just wasn't up to par
And they tried to better me.
Some say I'm cursed with a sin
This black skin I'm in,
It's nothing like what they show on the cinema
This seat's hotter than cinnamon.
This is one suit that cannot be unbuttoned.
No hanging up in the closet
It's not part of the custom.

This is adorned.
From the cradle to the grave.

My Soul Glows

Just as the rising sun dissipates darkness
With rays of light that arches,
Stretching forth from seas to forests
My soul glows.
Just as candles on top the mantle
With flickering flames that dance slow,
Casting shadows that intermingle
My soul glows.
Just as the oil lamp inside a cabin
When the fire place begins its crackling,
And the couple is smiling and laughing
My soul glows.
Just as the stars so far away
That shines even during the day,
But hidden like Amen Re
My soul glows.
See this little light of mine
I'm going to let it shine,
I said this little light of mine
Is just a spark of the divine.
Magical like the number nine
The glowing of my soul could blind,
You may need a welding face guard
Because I'm brilliant, I'm a quasar.
It's as if you faced God!
This is a sight to see

My soul so righteously free,
This cannot be sold to he
For my soul is the epitome of we.
Children of the sun… shine
Shine… shine… shine.
And glow as if you were blazing
Hot metal taking shape,
Glow as if you were the sun of righteousness
With no mistakes.
With healing in your wings
Your soul glows like U.F.O's,
Or neon signs when stores closed
Glow.
Just let your soul glow
I repeat, just let your soul glow!
Just as the stars
Just as the oil lamp,
Just as candles and the rising sun
Rise my son.
Rise my daughter
Go forth unto the world
Be a lighthouse for ships upon the waters.
Let your soul glow.

What Happened To Us

What happened to us?

Granddaddy passed
Then grandmama passed,
Our family went separate ways
Then drama came to pass.
Whoever thought when we were young
We'd drown our problems with a glass?
Or a bottle and a bag
Blowing smoke and flicking ash.
See our pain runs deep
Behind the scars and the scabs,
When we used to share laughs
Now our backs have stabs...
Wounds from a relative
More news and it's negative,
Only time we get together
Is at funeral processions it's...
Looking kind of grim
Because as young teenagers the cousins said
We'd be nothing like them.
Referring to our momma 'nem,
But truth is we grew to be identical
Another case of homonyms.

What happened to us?

From negros to niggers
Afro Americans,
From coloreds to blacks
African American.
We don't know who we are
History never taught us,
You think civilized men
Came out of a mountain called Caucasus?
In ships they brought us
In chains they bought us,
Insane and in vain
In God's name they slaughtered.
Loyalty was everywhere
From the fields to slave quarters,
For all the slaves that got away
Some slaves became martyrs.
Post traumatic stress we suffer
Willie Lynch syndrome we endure,
Heavy metals in Similac and Ensure
Got the blood in our bodies impure.

What happened to us?

Dreamy Nights We Share

With anticipations for my day to end
With anxiety for my night to begin,
With fervor, my bed I get in
With the expression of a childish grin.
My head nestled in a pillow so soft
My eyes shut as the lights are off,
My chest, my hands draped across
My dream, as I enter I'm lost.
It is here where I found my bliss
It is here where we met and kiss,
It is here that I often miss
It is here that I feel like this.
You have found me through time and space
You have such a beautiful face,
You healed a heart that ached
You have created a magical place.
The black that seems to bind
The stars which brilliantly shine,
The hand that's wrapped in mine
The journey through endless time.
Beyond the moon we go
Beyond the things I know,
Beyond the river that flow
Beyond our bodies that glow.

I Fell In Love

I fell in love with this beautiful queen
But she was the possession of another,
Something similar to a movie scene
Because I was employed by her mother.
How less of a man I felt inside
Knowing that I couldn't provide,
On the verge of struggling to survive
It could never be her and I.
My sister or lover, often I wondered
Was this the feeling of Ausar?
To her the thought may not sit well on her stomach
But still she's my shining star.
No woman made me as timid as she
Even those with decades on me,
Maybe it's the pureness of her soul I see
That has this fire inside, raging on me.
Her locs and pierced nose I suppose
Her slanted smile and her style,
With every step she came close, I froze
Transforming a man into a child.
I love her, I love her, I love her, I love her
These words I kept bottled up,
To not create discomfort for another
I stood still with no follow up.

A Day Of Remembrance

I can still remember that day
The day I first laid eyes upon you.
I cannot recall what style of clothing you wore nor color
But I do recall the emotions I felt.
For sight is a mere illusion
And what I felt was intense energy,
The kind that arcs across the sky and penetrates the ground
Causing the sands to melt.
So as I'm looking through the looking glass
Of my soul, what do I behold?
Beautiful energy emitting a beautiful human being
And not the other way around.
When you smiled my heart jumped for joy
Immediately dividing itself in two pieces
One for me… and one for you
Could this be love that I found?
Or did love find me?
As my outwards appearance resembled a still pond,
But on the inside was an ocean during typhoon season
Waves repeatedly crashing.
And as I sat on the opposing end
With my peripheral vision I watched you
Feeling drawn to you, attracted to you
A magnetic attraction.
When you spoke my ears began to hum
As if they were trying to tune into your frequency,

Never heard a voice as harmoniously as yours
Unless the whispers of the wind counts.
I thought to myself for a moment
That this must be the place where goddesses dwell,
But where are the trumpet blowers and most importantly
Why have you not been announced?
But you were and I had simply forgotten
It was the moment prior to me laying eyes on you,
Being caught up in one's own dream and fantasy
Can obscure the reality of it all.
The most beautiful in all the lands
And although these eyes can be deceived,
Your beauty was perceived by your energy
And on that day, I began to fall.

Epiphany

Last night as I gazed upon the moon
Contemplating life great mysteries,
So bright was she as the sun at noon
As I experienced an epiphany.
The end to worldly troubles revealed
In awe I sat and I watched,
The answers in which was never concealed
But forgotten perhaps or not.
The woman! Of course, it is her
The answer to the riddle,
The stars twinkled seeming to concur
And I laughed as a child just tickled.
Placing the woman back on the pedestal
And venerating her as a deity,
Love would freely and forever flow
Across continents and even seas.
When a woman loves, it fills you up
For it's the same as your favorite dish,
For all women to love is simply enough
Even world hunger would cease to exist.
If all women were loved and shed joyful tears
No one would die from thirst,
We could drink from these fountains for many of years
But not even one day from the tears of hurt.
Respecting women more, we would live in peace
Never experiencing battles and wars,

Because every man is the son of a woman, so grief
Is in a galaxy some place far.
I gazed upon the moon last night
Reflecting upon our troubles,
And I experienced a flash of insight
Which left me no longer befuddled.

Creativity Is Important In Education

*Creativity is important in education
It allows the mind to orchestrate symphonies,
With every note the mind composes
It produces music so beautifully.
Creativity is important in education
It transforms the simple mind into one that's complex,
Being able to understand the nouns and verbs
And decipher any subtle subtext.
 Creativity is important in education
It raises the intelligence of the mind like an exponent,
In addition to subtracting the limited perspective
It multiplies the skills held dormant.
Creativity is important in education
It thrusts the mind into the past,
It presents a futuristic way to travel through time
As it encompass a space so vast.
Creativity is important in education
It sculpts the mind and fashions wonderful works,
With colors so vibrant cascading leisurely
It saturates the earth.
Creativity is important in education
It strengthens and builds endurance,
Stamina increases with mental exercises
As it enables exercising prudence.
Creativity is important in education
It begins a cycle of actions and reactions,*

*Creating a bond between two or more substances
And love is the main attraction.*

Friendship

Whenever I needed a shoulder to lean on
You were there,
A special friend in the time of need
And you showed that you cared.
A friendship like ours
Weren't like any others,
We were so close in a way
It was like we were brothers.
I knew all the pain you went through
And all the tears that you shed,
All the thoughts that roamed your head
While lying in your bed.
I wish I could take away
All the hurt, pain and sorrow,
Away from your soul
Giving you a happier tomorrow.
But it's beyond my control or fate
You control your destiny,
The wonderful life that you've planned in your head
Can become reality.
So day by day I miss you
Hoping you'll soon get well,
Realizing you have a special friend waiting
With a lot of stories to tell.

In Memory Of You

In memory of all the love you gave
The most precious gift of all,
You shared and cared, nothing was spared
Will hatred and bitterness fall?
In memory of all the things you did
I couldn't do it by myself,
You helped and kept, I cried and wept
But never kept hope on the shelf.
In memory of how you inspired my dreams
And taught me to reach for the stars,
The thoughts were starts, I sat them apart
And dreams in reality were nothing but scars.
Mere instance of here today and gone tomorrow
But the memory of you will never,
I staggered and followed, battled with sorrows
But oh, how I'm so clever!
In memory of you, I give credit where due
And I admit, there are only a few,
Even though you're gone, I'm moving on
And in my memories, there's a memory of you.

Twin Soul Mates

In the eternal now did we not agree
That in this life time, you and me,
Would not be bound by land or sea
But in each other's arms we would be?
So why is it that when I awake
From day to day, when dawn escapes,
From the grips of dusk and its' fate
I reach for you and your warm embrace?
Only to be denied your sweetest touch
My aching heart severely crushed,
Perhaps it's punishment for a deed unjust
My tormented soul, it bleeds for us!
I will scour the earth and shall not rest
Beyond the valleys and mountains' crest,
To find you my love, I will forward press
Throughout this life and even death.
In the pits of hell I'll travel to
In fire and brimstones until I got through,
To let you know there's nothing I would not do
And I rather spend eternity in hell with you…
Than to be in heaven without you!

Loving You From Afar

There's just no other way to say this except
I... love you.
Three words I do not toss around as if I'm trying to win
A gold fish at a county fair know this, no Miss,
So bogus the claims of many, my focus when I spoke those
Three syllables were plenty,
Were hopes of it rising out the mud like a lotus
Sincerely.
Whenever you're near me let me tell you about
The experience I have,
In one word... heaven.
The apple of my eye, you're my eye candy, you're my eye pad.
I rest my eyes on you because you're easy on the eyes
Making my heart skip a beat,
Your voice is like the sweetest melodies on repeat.
I... love you.
These words I mumble and whisper
Like forgotten scriptures,
Too shy wishing I was brave and courageous
I'll just continue writing on these pages.
You really got a hold on me like
Call waiting or frozen assets,
I'm open with my flashlight in broad day
But trying to get passed that.
My heart torn from my chest like Aztecs.

I saw the sun, the moon, the mountains
 and the rivers last night listening to Az Yet.
If my lungs were to expel my last breath,
Could my eyes behold its' last vision?
The beauty of you, the different hues
Of love so true when a storm is coming, my refuge.
Bring me back to life with a kiss
From your sweet lips,
The magic of Tehuti, I'm a baboon
When I'm feeling like this.
I'm falling for you my darling
I'm calling your name in the morning,
As I'm yawning but I'm sighing
Damp pillows reveal last night crying.
Feels like I'm... dying.
What are wings without the wind?
What is knowledge without application?
What are nights without dreams?
What are kings without queens?
What is me without you?
I'll tell you... nothing.
It's no question if you're the one for me
But rather am I the one for you?
Separated by an invisible barrier
With a wonderful view.
Close but with enough distance arrows of rejection
Can't penetrate my bubble of protection.
How can you think highly of someone
With such low self esteem?

I mean the line should be read in between it seems.
Inside I'm bleeding.
This is the reason I'm pouring my soul as the ink is leaking
I'm seeking for a beacon,
I'm speaking what I'm speaking
Because I'm thinking it so frequent.
I... love you.
And it's no secret
Because it's secreted by my pores,
And absorbed by these walls
As I continue to love you from afar.

A Brother Forgotten

Bunk beds and laughter we shared
Scabs and tears we shed,
Running aimlessly free in the cornfield
Bath times after we've been fed.
The tree house that was never built
Playing karate in the front yard,
Saturday mornings watching cartoons
Purring kittens and barking dogs.
School clothes for the new year
Long walks to the bus stop,
Afternoons of noodles for lunch
Riding bikes with flip flops.
Board games, you win, you lose
Video games, I win, I lose,
Christmas eve we couldn't snooze
Play play fighting then call a truce.
Bags of candy from allowance spent
Ice cream sandwich with sandwich bread,
Kool aid cubes deliciously sweet
Jumping up and down on our beds.
Cartwheels and handstands
A race to decide the fastest,
Summer days on the ground we lay
Or turning flips on a mattress.
Bed time giggles with feet to face
Through the woods while eating berries,

Preschool scares subside with sips of water
Bus rides home feeling merry.
Memories fade when up in age
And distance is too great to cover,
The world's a bit colder when you're alone
Reminiscing of your forgotten brother.

Is It Alright If I Cry

If the entire day's stressful
And I couldn't figure why…
Is it alright if I cry?
If I gave it my all and fail
And no longer want to try…
Is it alright if I cry?
If I said, "I love you with all my heart."
And you replied with a sigh…
Is it alright if I cry?
If I'm dying of thirst
And my well runs dry…
Is it alright if I cry?
If life isn't worth living
And part of me wants to die…
Is it alright if I cry?

I'm Tired Y'all

I'm tired y'all.
Not physically, I'm talking about mentally and spiritually.
See it kills my spirit and weakens my soul
Because cops are out of control.
They're killing the youth; we don't get to grow old.
I'm tired y'all.
I'm tired of logging onto Facebook
And my friends saying, "Hey look!"
They just took the life of another one of our queens,
I can just imagine the pain as her mother screams,
"Not my baby!"
This is getting crazy.
I'm tired y'all.
These eyes of mine are all cried out.
How many times have we marched and cried out
"We want justice, we want justice!?"
And the system flips its' middle finger and says
All we have to offer is just this.
I'm tired y'all.
Tired of the marching and singing songs
Like… we shall overcome,
While they beat us like drums
That day never arrives
And we continue to lose lives.
I'm tired y'all.
You ever been so tired

Even small things agitate you?
Like even if you were speeding
The cop only pulled you over because he hates you.
Racial profiling, you know the charge
Driving while black,
I suffer from cop phobia because at any given moment
I could end up with holes in my back.
I'm tired y'all.
Everyday it's a struggle as a people being oppressed.
I confess, you hear our signal of distress,
We're depressed, our thoughts are suppressed.
We believe the media and the press
But not ourselves.
I'm tired y'all.
But I can gather up just enough energy
For one last fight,
One final blow
With all my might.
I'm tired of being tired
And I know that I'm right,
When I say we should stand up for our rights
And keep our enemies in sight.
My ancestors will give me strength.

When Kisses Were Cherished

When kisses were cherished
I'm talking about childhood conversations,
The sticky candy stained cheeks
And innocent faces.
Sweeter than cherries
Temptations for lip placements,
Right here on my right jaw
Oh my, oh my, oh my!
When kisses were cherished
They lasted for weeks and months,
I'm thinking about that kiss yesterday
I'm not thinking about lunch.
I'm full off love and sweet kisses
Teeth showing, big grinning,
My feet sweeping the ground
As I float by singing.
Kisses, kisses, kisses
Kiss me baby please,
I cherish your kisses
Like wind to the trees.
Beautiful summer's breeze
Lips big as bumble bees,
When I'm older I'll revert to memories
Of a younger me.
Happily skipping through hallways
You're on my mind all day,

When kisses were cherished
It meant the world always.

Teach Me

Teach me how to love
To love unconditionally with all my heart,
To know the difference between lust and love
My heavenly angel with your harp.
Play for me sweet melodies
Sing passionate songs to soothe the soul,
A voice as wondrous as the hummingbird
Captivate me as we stroll.
Teach me how to love
To love unselfishly my dear,
To love truthfully and honestly
As my consciousness is clear.
A student of love I am
I profess my lack of knowledge,
Teach me Oh master teacher
Teach me this thing called love.
Teach me how to love
To become love, teach me so,
That I may teach another
As we watch our love grow.

Let's Do It

You can start by stripping...
Stripping your mind of the things you thought you knew,
Expose your bare naked mind to sunlight information
Glistening like morning dew.
See whether or not what I say is true
Feel whether or not what I say is real,
Often times reality splits three ways
Like a banana peel.
Spread it for me...
The knowledge that is, needs to be passed around,
I like to start in the middle and work my way outward
I seem to cover more ground.
Look back at me...
I'm not the same person from the past,
Nothing remains the same
Not even our position has.
You love being on top...
But really, who enjoys rock bottom?
Our messages can be uplifting and inspiring
Just maintain this pace as if we're jogging.
Hold up, don't move...
Sometimes you have to be firm,
Never shy away from any opportunities
Where someone might learn.
Say what's on your mind
And know that opinions rarely count,

Present facts and data that can be researched
I'm talking about large amounts.
How does it feel…?
Does it leave your body drained?
Does it leave you completely exhausted?
Does it place a strain on your brain?
Did you come…
To the realization that maybe it's all worth it?
And that if only one person eyes are opened
Then surely he deserves it.
Let's do it…!
I'm talking about you and me,
Let's teach our people truth
Because the truth shall set them free!
But first…
You can start by stripping…
Stripping your mind away of the things you thought you knew,
Expose your bare naked mind to sunlight information
Glistening like morning dew.
See whether or not what I say is true
Feel whether or not what I say is real,
Often times reality split three ways
Like a banana peel.
Spread it for me.

She Is So Beautiful

Like the blue skies without a single cloud
Like your favorite song you sing out loud.
Like the spring time after winter storms
The love she feels when in his arms.
Like the rays from the sun upon her face
Like the gentle breeze she couldn't trace.
Like the quietness she finds at ponds
The peace she feels away from town.
Like the stars in heaven so far away
Like nature's calling, she must obey.
Like surrounded in darkness, she can't escape
The way she moves like the figure eight.
Like the bumble bee how it takes flight
Like the air you breathe on a mountain hike.
Like the ocean waves when it touch the shore
The sensations she gets, she can't ignore.
She is… she is… so beautiful.
She is… she is… so beautiful.
She is… she is… so beautiful.
She is… she is… so beautiful.

Ma

To the best mother a child could ask for
Ma, I love you so much,
And maybe it's because of the wonderful things you've
done or perhaps the love you have shown us.
The guidance you have given me as a child
To this day still I remember,
My mother, my mother, my mother
It is you they say I resemble.
My mother so kind and gentle
The sweetest woman on this earth,
Never will they find a momma like mine
No matter how far they search.
Ma, I love you so much
Even though I never say it,
As I always thought it was unnecessary
As long as a person displays it.
So throughout the years I hope my actions
Spoke the words I never,
I love you, I love you, I love you
Always and forever.
On this special day of yours
I wish you health, strength and life,
Along with happiness and joy
Plus love, peace and light!

I Want To Make You Smile

I've been noticing lately
It's like something heavy is pressed against your heart,
Like it's not enough time in the day
To finish the things you start.
I've seen how busy you are
With work and with the children,
You try so hard to please everyone
Now that's no way to be living.
Especially when you neglect yourself
I mean, who's taking care of you?
Who's making sure you're happy in life
While you do the things you do?
I just want you to pause for a moment
Relax, relate, release,
Let go of all the stress you're under
It's time for some peace.
My only purpose at this moment
Is to put a smile on your face,
So let's begin right away
And start with a warm embrace.
You are appreciated and loved
You are the reason the sun shines,
You are the reason the stars twinkle
You are truly divine.
You make the life of all others
So much easier to bare,

Although we may not say it
Better know that we care.
Just smile for me right now
Let me see it from ear to ear,
Let me hear that soft giggle of yours
And watch your worries disappear.
Smile like never before my love
Smile with the heart of a child,
Smile, smile and smile some more
I want to make you smile.

Sun Worshippers

We are children of the Sun
We are children of the Sun,
The elders smile as we play
Watching the children as we run.
From gates to galaxies
Blocks to binary star systems,
We travel like rays from the Sun
Dispersed diaspora like prisms.
We are children of the Sun
We are what you call wisdom,
Storing knowledge in many houses
Years go on, by the thousands.
We celebrate life and vitality
Erecting monuments of splendor,
Gentle giants for generations
From the golden globe's center.
Bathing in light, we're washed anew
Delightful view, come see,
Heru soaring the skies beyond the horizon
As boats sailing the seas.
We are children of the Sun
In all our majesty we shine victoriously,
We are shielded from iniquity
We are protected from our enemies.
As shadows flee when dawn breaks
A touch of warmth upon our face,

*We give praises, we give praises
Because we are shown grace*

His Wife Of Mine

Across this bed I lay
With memories from the past,
Softly I heard a voice say
It's your fault we didn't last.
With a tightening feeling in the chest
And the eyes becoming misty,
I ask this question under my breath
Do you ever at any time miss me?
I can still feel the warmth of your skin
And visualize your eyes engaging mine,
Though the fading image of your grin
Dissipates because of time.
Your love for me I wasn't sure
How was I to confirm such a thing?
When both our hearts were a bit impure
And suffered from a sting.
Perhaps the many years and a familiar face
Or just that day before November,
It's hard to say how we gotten to this place
But this place, I will always remember.
Like a swim off shore clasping hands
We rode the waves of life,
We didn't let go, it wasn't part of the plan
But the ocean was nothing nice.
We were awfully close to being perfect
Like a recipe minus an herb,

The bond we shared would often resurfaced
When years went by without a word.
The rekindling of flames to a roaring fire
We were masters of the element,
Blacksmiths to uncontrollable desires
In which we lost intelligence.
You never bid farewell which was far from fair
So closure was never close,
You had obligations and still you dared
To share with me the most.
Often I wondered if I entertained your gesture
Would our union be forever?
Or would we crack under the slightest pressure
Witnessing our tides rapidly sever?

This Thing Called Love

What is this thing called love?
Surely words cannot define it.
The entire world cannot contain it,
How then shall I explain it?
The heavens in its' vastness
The oceans in its' depth,
The mountains and the peaks there on
The wind and all its' breath.
The aches my heart does bare
Yearning to envision thou morning's face,
In bondage to the moonlit night, I am
Oh sun I beg your grace.
What is this thing called love?
It is passion that burns within,
For the flames cannot be quenched
It is passion that has no end.

Alone In A Crowded Room

We spend our whole life searching
Trying to define who we are,
Who am I? Just a soul striving to balance the scales of
Ma'at like a see-saw.
 I can see far... But not far enough in the future
To see where she are,
Excuse me... Where she is... Or where we are
Except in this crowded room right now beneath stars.
Well... Actually beneath this roof
And enclosed within these walls,
And... We're on opposite sides of this room
And according to universal laws.
Like attracts like
If I'm the effect then she's the cause,
She's playing a great part in this play we call life
So I guess I'm the applause.
And hold up... Pause
I see her and see no flaws,
I said, "I'm tired being alone."
And then she goes, "Awww."
She's empathetic and truthfully
Loneliness once in a while pays her a visit,
Holding her hands over her broken heart
Wishing someone could fix it.

I Care

The word love has been tainted.
It has been desecrated, misused and abused.
People now use the word love so freely
So freely, there are other words that I choose.
One word in particular
Which demonstrates compassion that's rare,
Is a word that is seldom used
And this word is care.
I care about the feelings you feel.
I care about the emotions you show.
I care about the thoughts on your mind.
I care about you more than you know.
I care about you to take the time
To ask, "How was your day?"
I care about this bond we share
Too much to let it slip away.
I care.
I care.
I care.

Bring Me A Dream

Anxiety builds as I prepare myself
For rest this evening,
Dear Mr. Sandman bring me a dream in which
I'm fully conscious while dreaming.
Dreaming of a hot summer's day
While I'm down by the stream and,
Enjoying time being spent with my queen
Watching the water dreening.
From her head to her neck
And collarbone, everything is serene and,
We're far from the projects and slums
Cops, sirens and screaming.
I said, dear Mr. Sandman bring me a dream
In which I'm dreaming,
Dreaming of a mountain top like Martin Luther King
With all the glory that he was seeing.
When my people are no longer bounded by slavery
They're all running free and
Free man, free woman, free child, free spirit
Free like the air that I'm breathing.
I said dear Mr. Sandman, dear Mr. Sandman
I have no time to be grieving,
I want to two step and have fun
Till it's no air left in my lungs and I start wheezing.
Dear Mr. Sandman
Bless me with a sweet dream like I'm sneezing,

From the pollen floating in the breeze
As I stroll through the Garden of Eden.
Is that you Adam? Is that you Eve?
Is that an apple that you're eating?
Put it down! Put it down! Put it down!
Where's Lilith when you need her?
 I want a dream so colossal
That I'm the universe and the stars are my atoms,
And the Milky Way is my pineal gland
Dear Mr. Sandman can you fathom?
Such a sweet dream as I jump for joy
Earth's axis tilt slightly from my spasm,
And the shooting star that arcs the sky
Is the result of a macrocosmic orgasm.
So the big "O" is The Big Bang
That's a sweet thing, sweet dream,
And dear Mr. Sandman
Do not place sand in my eyes that's just a bit mean.

I Live

From the very first moment that I exited my mother's womb, I cried out, "I live!"
Consumed by a world of death and darkness
I am life, I am light, I am heart for the heartless.
With charges of being three-fifths of a human
Still I display my godliness,
My departure does not exist.
My arrival standing on the outside of time's axis
Proves I'm revolutionary.
I live.
Surviving battles and wars, scarred mentally and physically,
Charred skin
But my soul still glows vividly.
Predicted to be extinct but my species on the Endangered list… Lives.
The genocide on my generation and those previously
Could not induce my extermination,
Only produced my determination.
I am a legend. I am the legacy of my ancestors.
As Tut Ankh Amen, I am the living image of our Lord.
The encore and the applaud. From near to abroad.
I am the North Star.

I Need What You Want

You say that you want love.
Well I need love.
I need love to circulate through my body
From the top of my head to the soles of my feet
And especially my heart like the fluid that's called...
Blood.
That's how bad I need love.
I need love.
I need love to fill my lungs as I inhale and I'll hold my
breath until I turn blue... for you.
See I don't want to exhale and give up this love
But if I pass out,
I'll be brought back to life by love
From you giving me mouth to mouth.
You say that you want to be happy.
Well I need to be happy.
I need to be happy like Ausar and Auset
Vishnu and Lakshmi, just relaxing.
With you by my side I'm smiling like Jack...
Nicholson when he played the joker in Bat...
Man... you just don't understand.
Everything you want... I need.
You say you want to be kissed passionately.
Well I need to kiss you passionately.
I need to feel your soft lips pressed against mine

As fireworks go off and sparks travel to the top of your
spine. Zion!
I'm talking about a kiss filled with so much passion,
Your knees start to buckle and you begin gasping...
"Take my breath away."
And it feels like you're crashing like the waves do in the
ocean but I'm your captain.
I promise to get you safe back to the shore
Mi amor.
You say you want someone to touch you.
Well I need to touch you.
I need to touch your smooth soft skin like
A naked canvas,
Who am I?
Just a new artist on campus.
I need to touch you like grandma walking up
Stairs holding on to the rail,
No...I need to touch you like I was blind
And your body was covered with Braille. Yeah.
You say that... What you really want is someone to trust.
Well I need you to trust me.
If the earth begin to quake and the buildings fell
I'd push you out the way and let them crush me.
Trust me.
If you were going in battle against the whole world
I'd be by your side even if my only weapon was a butter
knife all corroded and rusty. Trust me.
Before they touch you they have to touch me.
You say you want honesty.

Well I need honesty too.
Honestly, in all honesty, I need someone to be honest to.
The world is filled with liars and deceivers and it's hard to know who is true,
So as I maneuver through the crowd it's hard to decipher
Who is who. But you.
Because of the vibrations you give off I'm sure.
Honestly I never knew a heart that was so pure.
You say you want commitment.
Well I need commitment.
If I was your lawyer and you were on trail
I wouldn't stop fighting until you got acquitted.
Even if they gave you life, every single day I'd come
Pay you a visit.
Then strategize a plan to break you out
Yeah it's a felony but I'd risk it.
How's that for commitment?
You say you want respect.
Well I feel the need to respect you.
R-E-S-P-E-C-T
There's no way I'd ever neglect you.
I feel the need to respect you like the
Queen and goddess you are,
I feel the need to bow and worship you
Because you shine like a star. Im Sirius.
Today, I know men don't respect women
Like they should,
It's all about being a manly man
And the hardest out the hood.

But see… instead of degrading our women with
Derogatory statements,
I'm setting forth a path of respect
That's concrete like pavements.
Come walk with me.
Because everything you want… I need.

About the Author

Neter Ankh Hotep-El has been writing poetry as far back as he can remember. He has won many contests and recognition for his poems. His passion for writing has never subsided through the years as he has written also short plays, movie scripts and songs.

Unspoken Words, Beautifully Written is Neter's published poetry book which is being followed by a three series children's book collection, soon to be published.

www.ingramcontent.com/pod-product-compliance
Lightning Source LLC
Chambersburg PA
CBHW071457070426
42452CB00040B/1554